Helping Children See Jesus

ISBN: 978-1-64104-017-4

FORGIVENESS
New Testament Volume 10: Life of Christ Part 10

Author: Ruth B. Greiner
Illustrator: Frances H. Hertzler
Colorization courtesy of Good Life Ministries
Typesetting and Layout: Morgan Melton, Patricia Pope

© 2018 Bible Visuals International
PO Box 153, Akron, PA 17501-0153
Phone: (717) 859-1131
www.biblevisuals.org

All rights reserved. No part of this publication may be reproduced, stored in a retrieval system or transmitted in any form by any means, electronic, mechanical, photocopy, recording or otherwise, without the prior permission of the publisher, except as provided by USA copyright law.

RELATED ITEMS

To access related items (such as activities, memory verse posters and translated texts) please visit our web store at shop.biblevisuals.org and enter 1010 in the search box on the page.

FREE TEXT DOWNLOAD

To access a FREE printable copy of the teaching text (PDF format) in English or other available languages, enter S1010DL in the search box. Add the item to your cart, and use coupon code XTACSV17 at checkout. Once your order is processed you will receive an email with a link to the free download.

And be ye kind one to another, tenderhearted, forgiving one another, even as God for Christ's sake hath hath forgiven you.

Ephesians 4:32

© Bible Visuals International Inc

Lesson 1
WOMAN IN THE HOUSE OF SIMON

NOTE TO THE TEACHER

The forgiveness of God passes human understanding. There is no sin so great or so vile that God cannot forgive. But even the smallest sin needs also to be forgiven by God.

The New Testament word *forgiveness* means "to send off" or "away." The idea is that sin, when it is forgiven, is separated from the sinner. This does not mean, however, that God simply overlooks sin. He has said, "The soul that sinneth, it shall die" (Ezekiel 18:4, 20). And, according to Leviticus 17:11, "It is the blood (upon the altar) that maketh an atonement for the soul." (See also Leviticus 4:35.) So it is clear that God requires a penalty for sin.

For hundreds of years before the coming of God the Son to earth, God the Father accepted the sacrificing of animals as substitutes. The sinner brought his animal to the tabernacle. It was slain and then burned upon the altar. Thus the sentence of death was paid by the death of the animal. Because man sinned repeatedly, he had to bring sacrifices again and again.

All of that was changed, however, after the death of the Lord Jesus Christ. The blood of bulls and goats and lambs is no longer acceptable to God. When God the Son gave His own blood willingly, He died in the place of every sinner. God the Father has accepted that one perfect sacrifice as a substitute for all the sins of the whole world (Hebrews 10:4-14).

Let it be remembered:

1. The penalty for sin is death (Romans 6:23).
2. The penalty must be paid (Hebrews 9:22).
3. The Lord Jesus paid the penalty with His blood (1 Peter 2:24).
4. By believing in the Lord Jesus Christ we receive forgiveness for our sins (Matthew 26:28).

In this series we shall learn in lesson one that *God can forgive sinners;* in lesson two, that *children of God must forgive those who sin against them;* and in lesson three, *that if someone has something against us, we must ask his forgiveness.*

You–and your pupils, also–should write the following truths in your notebooks under the heading FORGIVENESS:

1. The *origin* of forgiveness: *The love and grace of God.*
2. The *basis* of forgiveness: *The sacrifice of Christ.*
3. The *result* of forgiveness: *The death penalty of the sinner is paid.*
4. Two things involved in forgiveness:
   (1) *The justice of God is satisfied.*
   (2) *The sinner is separated from his sin.*

God demands full payment for sin before He can forgive!

Scripture to be studied: Luke 7:36-50

The *aim* of the lesson: To show that God is able and willing to forgive any sinner.

What your students should *know:* God can forgive sinners because His Son paid the penalty for sin–death.

What your students should *feel:* Unhappy over one's sins; the need to be forgiven.

What your students should *do:* Believe Jesus is the Son of God and receive Him as Saviour.

Lesson outline (for the teacher's and students' notebooks):

1. Seeking Jesus (Luke 7:36-37).
2. Finding Jesus (Luke 7:37-38).
3. Forgiven by Jesus (Luke 7:39-49).
4. Joy from Jesus (Luke 7:50).

The verse to be memorized:

And be ye kind one to another, tenderhearted, forgiving one another, even as God for Christ's sake hath forgiven you. (Ephesians 4:32)

THE LESSON

1. SEEKING JESUS
Luke 7:36-37

Show Illustration #1

A sad and lonely woman walked down the street of a city of Galilee. Nobody wanted to walk with her. No one cared to talk to her. The people in the city knew that she was a sinful woman.

She, too, knew that she was sinful. Oh, if only she had not done such wicked things! She wanted to forget her past, but she could not. Every day she was reminded of her evil deeds.

Even the people who were once her friends now turned their backs to her or ridiculed her as she walked by. She felt alone and helpless. She knew that the penalty for sin is death.

There was one Person, however, and only one, who seemed different from everyone else. He talked differently–not with scorn but with love. The woman had heard of some of the things He had said as He spoke to great crowds. One thing He had said was: "Come to Me, all of you who are weary and overburdened, and I will give you rest . . . Learn from Me, for I am gentle and lowly in heart and you will find rest for your souls" (Matthew 11:28-29).

She was overburdened–overburdened with sin. She could not rest because of her sins–and because of the thought of the penalty for sin. But this One, Jesus, had told people to come to Him for rest. Would He be willing to help her, even though she was a sinner?

2. FINDING JESUS
Luke 7:37-38

She had heard that Jesus had been invited to eat at the home of a man named Simon. Simon was a Pharisee, and Pharisees despised sinful women like her. Although she knew this, she wanted to get close to the Lord Jesus. She had not been invited to eat at the home of Simon. Nevertheless she hoped to step inside the open doorway, as other people did, to watch Jesus as He ate.

Quietly she followed others who went into the home of Simon. She saw Simon welcoming Jesus–but not with the kiss on the cheek which was usually given to honored guests. That seemed strange. She expected someone would bring a basin of water to wash the dust from the sandaled feet of the guests, for that was the custom. But Simon did not bother about that either. Nor did he–as was proper–anoint with oil the head of his important Visitor.

The woman could not understand it. Surely Simon must have known that Jesus was a great teacher. How could he be so rude to a guest?

She watched as Jesus and the other guests were led to their places at the table. In that land the people leaned on couches with their heads toward the table and their feet away from it as they ate their meal.

Show Illustration #2

The woman crept quietly behind Jesus and stood at His feet, crying. She did not look around. She was not concerned about what the others thought. The closer she was to Him, the more she realized how sinful she was. Oh, how she cried! She knew that she, sinner that she was, was not worthy to be near the Lord Jesus. She cried and cried so much that soon the feet of Jesus were all wet–wet enough to be washed with her tears. Having no towel, she bent down and dried His feet with her long hair. She kissed his feet again and again. Then she took a bottle from the folds of her dress. Lovingly she poured sweet-smelling ointment from the bottle onto the feet of Jesus.

3. FORGIVEN BY JESUS
Luke 7:39-49

Show Illustration #3

All the while Simon the Pharisee had been watching her. He had seen all her actions, and he did not like what he saw. He was disgusted. *What is she doing in my house?* he thought to himself. *She is a sinful woman. Jesus should send her away. If He is really a prophet, He should know what a sinful woman she is.* Simon wanted to get the woman out of his house.

The Lord Jesus, knowing exactly what Simon was thinking, said, "Simon, there is something I want to say to you." Then Jesus told him this brief story: "There was once a man who was owed money by two people. One owed money equal to wages for 500 days. The other owed the equal of wages for 50 days. But neither of them could pay what they owed. So the man graciously forgave both of them. Tell Me, Simon, which one do you suppose loved him the most after that?"

"I suppose the one whom he forgave the most loved him the most," Simon replied.

"You are right," said Jesus. Then turning to the woman He said to Simon, "Look! See this woman kneeling here? I came to your house and you did not offer Me water to wash the dust from My feet. But she has washed My feet with her tears and dried them with her hair. You gave Me no kiss of greeting as is the custom. But from the moment I came in she has continually kissed My feet. You did not anoint My head with oil but she has covered My feet with ointment."

By this time Simon should have been very much ashamed of himself, but he said nothing.

Jesus continued: "That is why I tell you, Simon, that her sins which are many, are forgiven, for she has shown Me so much love. But the man who has little to be forgiven has only a little love to give."

Then to the woman Jesus said, "Your sins are forgiven."

Could it be true? She had heard Him say the word *forgiven*. And He had said it to her! She found it hard to believe that her sins were forgiven–not only one sin but *all* of her sins. She would not have to think about them again. She was forgiven of her sinful past–forgiven by the Son of God Himself. No longer was there sadness on her face. Her heart was filled with joy. It did not matter to her that the other men at the table were whispering among themselves. If she had listened she would have heard them say: "Who is this Man, who even forgives sins?" They did not believe that Jesus is the Son of God and that He has power to forgive sins. Nor did they believe that anyone could have so much love that He would forgive a sinful woman.

4. JOY FROM JESUS
Luke 7:50

Speaking again to the woman, Jesus said, "Your faith has saved you. Go in peace."

Show Illustration #4

The woman left the house. Her expensive ointment was gone. But that didn't matter. Now she could lift her head and smile again. Her sins were forgiven. God would never hold them against her any more. (See Hebrews 10:17.) She was pure and clean in His sight.

Is *your* heart pure and clean in the sight of God? Have your sins been forgiven? No sin is too great or wicked for God to forgive. But perhaps you say, "I have never done a very great sin." That is the way Simon the Pharisee felt. He did not think that he had done great sins. But he had no sympathy at all for the woman. He was proud. So, in the sight of God, he needed to be forgiven just as the woman did. Even the smallest sin is wicked in the sight of our holy God.

The penalty of sin is death. The penalty must be paid. The Lord Jesus Christ paid your penalty by His death. If you believe Him to be the Son of God and will receive Him as your Saviour, you too will have forgiveness of sin.

Lesson 2
SEVENTY TIMES SEVEN

NOTE TO THE TEACHER

The forgiveness of God is complete and far greater than human forgiveness. God, who is perfect and holy, is able to forgive a guilty sinner because sin's penalty, death, was paid by our Lord Jesus Christ.

In this lesson it will be your privilege to teach the wonderful truth of forgiveness as it relates to the believer in Christ. Because God in His marvelous love has forgiven us, we who are children of God ought to forgive one another. Our love for Christ should be shown in our relationship with fellow believers–in our attitude to those who wrong us. There should be no limit to our forgiveness, even as there is no limit to the forgiveness of God.

Ask God to create in you a loving and forgiving nature, teacher, so that you will be an example to your students in this important characteristic of the Christian life.

We mentioned before that the New Testament word *forgiveness* means "to send off" or "away." Another thought is included in the word forgiveness and it appears in this lesson. *Forgiveness* also means "to loose." The king had compassion on the servant who owed him 10,000 talents and "loosed him, and forgave him" (Matthew 18:27). The sins of the sinful woman (about whom we studied in the first lesson were forgiven her–she was separated from her sin. As the servant (in this second lesson) was forgiven (loosed) from his huge debt, so we are to forgive those who wrong us–forgive them times without number. How is this possible? By the power of the indwelling Christ. He enables us to do that which is quite the reverse of our human nature.

If your students understand the meanings of the terms *talents* and *pence* in Matthew 18:24 and 28, it will help them to see the wickedness of the man whom the king forgave. A talent was probably worth about 6,000 pence. So 10,000 talents would be 60,000,000 pence. A pence equaled wages for one day. So the first man was forgiven the wages of 60,000,000 days! Then he refused to forgive the man who owed him only 100 pence–or wages for 100 days. Imagine that!

Scripture to be studied: Matthew 18:1-6, 21-35; Mark 9:30-37; Luke 9:44-48; Mark 10:35-37

The *aim* of the lesson: To teach that because God in His love has forgiven us, our love for Christ should be shown in our forgiving fellow Christians.

What your students should *know*: Children of God must forgive those who sin against them.

What your students should *feel*: A loving and forgiving spirit toward others.

What your students should *do*:
  Unsaved: Experience God's forgiveness by receiving Christ as Saviour.
  Saved: Forgive those who have wronged them.

Lesson outline (for the teacher's and students' notebooks):
1. Who is greatest in Heaven? (Mark 9:30-34; Luke 9:44-46).
2. To be great, one must be humble (Matthew 18:1-6; Mark 9:35-37; Luke 9:47-48).
3. Forgive others because of God's forgiveness (Matthew 18:21-27).
4. Failure to forgive is sin (Matthew 18:28-35).

The verse to be memorized:

And be ye kind one to another, tenderhearted, forgiving one another, even as God for Christ's sake hath forgiven you. (Ephesians 4:32)

THE LESSON

The Lord Jesus had just taught His disciples some amazing truths. He had explained that He would be delivered into the hands of men and that they would kill Him. After His death, He would rise the third day. What had He said? That He, God the Son, would die. He would not stay dead. He would live again. That seems perfectly clear. But do you know what? The disciples did not understand what Jesus said. And, the Bible tells us, "they were afraid to ask Him."

1. WHO IS GREATEST IN HEAVEN?
Mark 9:30-34; Luke 9:44-46

Having been in company with the Lord Jesus so long, you would suppose that they would have eagerly asked Him questions about what He had taught them. But no! Instead, when those 12 disciples were alone, they had an argument.

Show Illustration #5

Even Peter, James and John–the three who on special occasions were closest to Jesus–argued. Did the twelve argue about the teaching the Lord Jesus had just given them? No! Did anyone hear what they quarreled about? No! At least, as far as the disciples knew, no one heard them.

In a house in Capernaum, the disciples were surprised. The Lord Jesus greeted them by asking, "What were you arguing about on the way?" He hadn't *heard* their quarrel, but He *knows* everything that happens.

The disciples were embarrassed. They did not like it that the Son of God knew that they had been disputing among themselves. But their faces must have shown that they hated to think of the thing about which they had been arguing. In His pure light, their own pride was revealed, and pride is sin. For along the way they had been disputing among themselves which of them would be greatest in Heaven. They had not been talking about the truths that He had taught them: that He, God the Son would be captured by men; that He would die; that He would rise again. No! All they were concerned about was which of them would be greatest in Heaven.

2. TO BE GREAT, ONE MUST BE HUMBLE
Matthew 18:1-6; Mark 9;35-37
Luke 9:47-48

But Jesus did not call out the name of one who would be the greatest. Instead He said: "If any man wants to be first, he must he last, and a servant of all."

Show Illustration #6

Calling a small child to Him, He put His arm around the child and said to the

– 20 –

disciples: "Unless you turn to God from your sins and become as little children, you'll never even get into the kingdom of Heaven. The man who can be as humble as this little child will be greatest in the kingdom of Heaven. Anyone who welcomes one child like this for My sake, is welcoming Me and caring for Me." Jesus loved children. And He wished that His disciples would be humble as the children were.

How ashamed the disciples must have been! The Lord Jesus had answered the question about who would be the greatest in Heaven. To be great in the eyes of God, He said, one must be willing to be the least . . . the last . . . a servant of others. Jesus had settled their quarrel quickly.

But this was not the only time that the disciples had argued. Sometimes Peter did things that the other disciples did not like. And there must have been times when John, and James, and Philip and Nathanael said things to each other that were wrong. Andrew may have done things and said things to his brother Peter that were not right. Perhaps all of the disciples found it difficult to forgive and forget.

3. FORGIVE OTHERS BECAUSE OF GOD'S FORGIVENESS
Matthew 18:21-27

Peter was troubled. One day he asked Jesus, "Lord, how often am I to forgive my brother who sins against me? Seven times?"

"No," Jesus answered, "not seven times, but 70 times seven."

Peter could hardly believe what he heard. Seventy times seven was 490 times! The Lord Jesus was actually telling Peter to keep on forgiving those who offended him, not even counting the number of offenses. Peter could not imagine how he could forgive his brother Andrew or anyone else that often! *Why* should he continually forgive another?

Jesus knew the thoughts of Peter. He knew that Peter did not really grasp what true forgiveness is. He wanted Peter to understand that he should forgive others because God had forgiven him. So Jesus told him this story:

Show Illustration #7

There was a king who had many servants. One of the servants owed the king much, much money (10,000 talents). The king demanded that servant to pay back his debt.

"O King!" the servant cried, "I cannot pay you right now. I do not have the money."

The king commanded his men, "Sell him as a slave! Sell his wife! Sell his children! Sell everything he has! Bring that money to me to pay his debt!"

The servant fell down at the feet of the king, crying, "Oh, be patient with me, Your Majesty, and I will pay you back everything I owe."

"Loose him! Set him free!" the king commanded. "He does not have to pay back his debt. I forgive him."

"Forgiven! I am forgiven!" the servant cried. "I do not have to pay back the money. I do not have to be sold as a slave!" He hurried home to tell his wife the news.

4. FAILURE TO FORGIVE IS SIN
Matthew 18:28-35

Show Illustration #8

On his way, he met another servant. He remembered that this man had borrowed a little money from him (100 pence). Grabbing the man by the throat, he shouted, "You owe me some money! I demand that you pay me back right now!"

The fellow servant fell to his knees and begged, "Please wait a little longer and I will pay you back what I owe."

"No! I will not wait any longer. I will have you thrown into prison!"

And that is just what he did.

Some of the other servants who saw what had happened, rushed to tell the king.

The king called the servant whom he had forgiven. "You wicked servant!" he exclaimed. "I forgave you your tremendous debt when you begged me to do so. You should have had pity on your fellow servant as I had on you. You are a wicked man! Now you must pay back all your debt!" And he had that servant thrown into jail.

As Peter listened to the story he began to understand what Jesus had been teaching. As God forgives our sins–our many, many sins–so we ought to forgive the few wrong things that others do to us (or the wrongs that we *imagine* they do to us).

Do you find it hard to forgive someone who has wronged you? Is it difficult for you to forgive a person again and again and again? To the children of God is given this command: "Be ye kind one to another, tenderhearted, forgiving one another, even as God for Christ's sake hath forgiven you" (Ephesians 4:32). God has willingly forgiven all your sin. As the king loosed his servant who owed the huge debt, God has loosed you from your sin. You are forgiven. Are you willing to forgive the wrongs of those who sin against you? The Lord Jesus who lives within you, will help you. Ask Him to give you a loving and forgiving spirit.

Perhaps you have never known the forgiveness of God in your life. You know that God is holy–God is perfect. You know that you are a sinner. You know that sin must be punished. Do you know that the Lord Jesus Christ is the Son of God? He, the perfect One, took upon Himself, when He died, all of your sin. He took your punishment. And He is waiting this moment to loose you from your sin. He is ready to say to you, "You are forgiven!" The moment you recognize the Lord Jesus as the Son of God and receive Him as your Saviour, you will know the joy of His forgiveness. Then you will be able, with His help, to forgive those who wrong you.

Lesson 3
ANGER AGAINST A BROTHER

NOTE TO THE TEACHER

In this series on forgiveness, we have learned:

(1) God can forgive the sinner because His Son paid the penalty for sin–death.

(2) Those who are forgiven sinners should be willing–with all humility–to forgive those who wrong them.

In this lesson we learn another important truth about forgiveness:

(3) If a believer sins against another, he must quickly seek the forgiveness of that one whom he has wronged. Then God will forgive him.

You will see in this portion the importance of examining our hearts when we approach God, acknowledging our sin and our guilt. The sin of murder is a great sin. But in our study we shall learn that God sees the heart. And what He sees may be as vile as the act of murder.

Ask God, dear teacher, to help you to learn:

(1) To be quick to judge yourself.
(2) To be slow to judge others.
(3) To be quick to seek forgiveness of those you have wronged.
(4) To be quick to confess your sins to God, claiming His forgiveness.
(5) To be ready to forgive others.

Once you have learned these truths, it will be simple for you to teach them to your pupils.

It is important to remember that final judgment for any sin is in the hands of God alone.

Scripture to be studied: Matthew 5:21-26

The *aim* of the lesson: To show that when a Christian wrongs another, he must immediately ask forgiveness.

What your students should *know*: If they have wronged anyone, they must ask his forgiveness.

What your students should *feel*: Concerned if one has wronged another.

What your students should *do*: As soon as possible, ask forgiveness of the one you have wronged.

Lesson outline (for the teacher's and students' notebooks):

1. Anger, like all sin, must be judged (Matthew 5:21).
2. God's severe punishment for sin (Matthew 5:22).
3. God requires Christians to forgive others (Matthew 5:23-24).
4. Forgiveness must be immediate (Matthew 5:25-26).

The verse to be memorized:

And be ye kind one to another, tenderhearted, forgiving one another, even as God for Christ's sake hath forgiven you. (Ephesians 4:32)

THE LESSON

The Lord Jesus sat on the hillside with His disciples. He had some important things to teach. As He taught, they listened. He always said the right thing. He never let anything slip out of His mouth that He should not have said. His own life was a perfect example to His followers.

1. ANGER, LIKE ALL SIN, MUST BE JUDGED
Matthew 5:21

After Jesus had talked of other things, He began to speak to the disciples about the Law of God. He said, "You have heard that it was said to people in the old days, 'You shall not commit murder, and anyone who does must be brought to judgment.'"

Show Illustration #9

The disciples understood what Jesus meant. They knew that when a person broke the sixth commandment (You shall not commit murder) he had to appear before the Sanhedrin–a council of 70 men–to be judged and sentenced to death by stoning.

The disciples had never killed anyone. Why was Jesus talking to them about this particular law and the punishment for murder?

Jesus added something that must have shocked each disciple. He said: "I say to you, that anyone who is angry with his brother must be brought to judgment."

James knew that at times he had been angry at his brother John. Peter thought of the times when he had been angry with Andrew, his brother. The other disciples knew that Jesus was talking to them, too, for when He used the word *brother,* He did not mean only members of their families, He meant neighbors and others whom they knew. The disciples had been angry many times. But did they deserve to be punished simply for being angry?

2. GOD'S SEVERE PUNISHMENT FOR SIN
Matthew 5:22

The Lord Jesus continued, "Anyone who calls his brother 'Raca' (meaning "empty head," a person at whom one would spit) is in danger of being brought to judgment before the court. And whoever says to another person 'you fool!' (meaning "a wicked person," someone who does not believe in God–see Psalm 14:1) shall be in danger of hell fire."

Show Illustration #10

The people of that day knew of the Valley of Hinnom outside the city of Jerusalem. There rubbish, filth and dead animals were thrown into a fire that burned continually. It was a solemn reminder to all who saw it of the unending punishment of the wicked. But the punishment of which Jesus spoke was far worse than that fire in the Valley of Hinnom. It was a punishment that would last forever, separating the sinner from God and from all that is good and pure and holy.

What was Jesus telling the disciples? This: "For ages and ages you have been taught that the sixth commandment–You shall not commit murder–is broken only by the murderer, and he is judged in the proper way before the council. But I say to you that the spirit of the law is broken when a person becomes angry. For anger leads to hatred and hatred leads to murder. God, the Judge who knows all things–even hidden things of the heart–will judge the sinner and punish him accordingly."

How could the disciples ever escape the terrible punishment which they deserved because of the anger and hatred which they themselves had shown? There was only one way. They would have to confess their sins to be forgiven.

3. GOD REQUIRES CHRISTIANS TO FORGIVE OTHERS
Matthew 5:23-24

Jesus explained what they should do by saying, "If, when you are bringing your gift of sacrifice to the altar, you suddenly remember that your brother has something against you, you must leave your gift at the altar. Go and make peace with your brother, and then come back and offer your gift."

Show Illustration #11

Peter, Andrew, James and John, as well as the other disciples, understood perfectly what Jesus meant. The very next time any one of them would go to the temple (the place where God was worshiped) to offer a lamb as a sacrifice for his sins, he would bring it into the court of the temple as he had always done. He would stand at the rails that separated him from the court of the priests. There he would wait for the priest to come and take his gift to be sacrificed on the altar. But if suddenly he remembered that he had been angry with someone, or perhaps had sinned against him in another way, what was he to do? Should he offer his sacrifice to God? No! Jesus said he was to leave his gift right there in the temple, go find the one he had offended, confess that he had sinned against him and ask his forgiveness. Having done that, he could come back and offer his gift to God. Then God would willingly accept his offering and forgive his sins.

4. FORGIVENESS MUST BE IMMEDIATE
Matthew 5:25-26

The Lord Jesus was talking to the disciples about breaking *the laws which God had given.* But what about *the laws that were made by men*? Suppose one of the disciples had broken one of the man-made laws of the land. His enemy insisted that he was in the wrong and threatened to take him to a court of law. Jesus wanted the disciples to know what to do in such a case. So He said to them: "If someone sues you and is about to take you to a court of law about some wrong he claims you have done, go with him. Make friends with him quickly, while you are going with him to court. Otherwise he may hand you over to the judge. The judge in turn will have you thrown into prison. Believe Me, you will never get out again until you have paid the last penny."

Show Illustration #12

The disciples had a lot to think about. Now they had to go out and put into practice what Jesus had taught them. Today we might put it into other words like these: "Peter, be quick to say you are sorry. John, do not be proud and refuse to ask for forgiveness. James, do not argue even though you may think you are always right. Andrew, be ready and willing to forgive Peter. Philip, do not get angry when Nathanael says something you do not like."

But wait a minute! Jesus was not talking to His disciples only. The very words He said to them were put down for us to read and obey.

He says to us now: (*Teacher:* Use any appropriate names) "Mary, be quick to say you are sorry. John, do not be afraid to ask forgiveness of someone you have wronged. Carlos, do not argue because you think you are always right. Daniel, be quick to judge yourself and not so quick to judge others. Becky, be ready and willing to forgive your sister. David, do not get angry with your brother or your friend when he says something you do not like."

We are told that in the early days of Christianity, before going to church brothers and sisters and fathers and mothers would ask forgiveness of one another for anything they had done wrong. What a fine thing! But we should not wait to ask forgiveness just before going to church. We should ask forgiveness as soon as we have done wrong. How soon? Immediately! "Let not the sun go down upon your wrath" (Ephesians 4:26) is a clear command of God. You cannot truly worship God at the close of the day if you are angry at someone–or if you have wronged him in some other way. So be quick to go to the one you have wronged and ask his forgiveness. Then, when you confess your sin to God, He, the Faithful One, will forgive you (1 John 1:9).

Today we do not bring a lamb as a sacrifice to God. The Lord Jesus, the Lamb of God who takes away the sin of the world, is our Sacrifice. He has died, taking the punishment for our sin. When we receive Him as Saviour, our sins are forgiven. The believer is required to "offer the sacrifice of praise to God continually . . . giving thanks to His name" (Hebrews 13:15). But you cannot praise God if there is something in your life which needs to be forgiven.

Lesson 4
FORGIVENESS

The *aim* of the lesson: To show that God has provided forgiveness of sin for all unsaved and for Christians when they fall into sin.

What your students should *know*: Forgiveness of sins cost God His only Son, and cost Christ His own life.

What your students should *feel*: A deep desire to experience God's forgiveness.

What your students should *do*:
 Unsaved: Receive Jesus Christ as Saviour from sin.
 Saved: Confess any sin to God.

Lesson outline (for the teacher's and students' notebooks):
1. God provides forgiveness today through Jesus Christ (Romans 5:8; Isaiah 53:6).
2. God provided forgiveness for those who lived before the Lord Jesus (Leviticus 16).
3. God provides forgiveness for Christians when they confess their sins to Him (1 John 1:9).

The verse to be memorized:

And be ye kind one to another, tenderhearted, forgiving one another, even as God for Christ's sake hath forgiven you. (Ephesians 4:32)

NOTE TO THE TEACHER

Forgiveness of sin is a priceless gift from God. While it is free to us, it cost God the very best that He had. It cost Him His own dear Son. To secure our forgiveness God gave His Son as a sacrifice for our sins. Before teaching this lesson ask yourself, teacher: "Do I fully appreciate the provision of God for the forgiveness of my sins?" Ask God to give you a deeper understanding of this marvelous work of His grace.

In this lesson you will stress three matters:

(1) The forgiveness of sin which God has provided for the unsaved today.

(2) The forgiveness of sin which God provided for those who lived before the Lord Jesus came to earth.

(3) The forgiveness of sin which God has provided for Christians when they fall into sin.

REVIEW

In this series we have studied what the Bible says about *forgiveness*.

From what story did we learn that *God can forgive sinners*? Think! But do not answer aloud.

Next, we learned that *children of God must continually forgive those who sin against them*. Do you remember what story Jesus told to prove that?

Last, we learned that *when we sin against a person, we must immediately seek his forgiveness*.

We need three people to tell us these three lessons. (*Teacher:* Show the three pictures on page 13. If your pupils cannot tell the stories, you will do so.)

 ### Show Illustration #13a

The woman in the house of Simon the Pharisee knew that she was a sinner. She knew that the penalty for sin is death. She was sorry for her sin. And she went to the One–the only One–who could say, "Your sins are forgiven!" He, the Lord Jesus Christ, by giving Himself as the perfect sacrifice for sin, became *her* substitute.

The Lord Jesus is *our* substitute sacrifice. When we receive Him as Saviour, we are born into the family of God at once–and are His children forever. As it was with the woman, so it is with us. *God can–and does!–forgive sinners.*

Show Illustration #13b

What should be the attitude of the child of God when someone sins against him? There is only one answer to that: forgive him, even as God, for Christ's sake has forgiven you.

How often should a child of God forgive another? Time and time and time again–times without number.

You remember that the man, whom the king forgave of the tremendous debt, grabbed his fellow servant (who owed him only a comparatively small amount of money) and threw him in jail. He had been forgiven a great deal. He would not forgive a little bit. The Holy Spirit of God is grieved when a forgiven sinner refuses to forgive another. (See Ephesians 4:30-32.) *Children of God must continually forgive those who sin against them.*

Show Illustration #13c

And if we sin against someone else, what should we do? As Jesus explained, we should be like a man who brings his sacrifice to the temple and remembers that he has sinned against someone. He should leave his sacrifice and go at once to the one whom he has offended and ask his forgiveness. Immediately, as soon as we possibly can, *we should go to the person against whom we have sinned and beg his forgiveness.* Then, and then only, can we truly worship God.

THE LESSON

Did anyone ever give you a gift all wrapped up and securely fastened? Were you curious? Did you open the gift, expecting to find only one thing, and find three, four, or even five things? What a surprise!

1. GOD PROVIDES FORGIVENESS TODAY THROUGH JESUS CHRIST
Romans 5:8; Isaiah 53:6

God has given a gift to us. It is not the kind of gift you can see. But it is the greatest gift you can ever receive. It is a priceless gift. It is *the gift of salvation*. I trust you have already received this gift. If you have believed that the Lord Jesus Christ is the Son of God and have received Him as Saviour, then you have received salvation, the gift of God. "By grace you are saved through faith; and that not of yourselves, it is the gift of God–not of works, lest any man should boast" (Ephesians 2:8-9).

Salvation is such a wonderful gift that we cannot really tell all that there is to know about it. But if you were able to unwrap the gift of salvation, as you unwrap other gifts, you would find many happy surprises. In the gift of salvation God has provided a number of wonderful things. Some Bible students have counted at least 33 additional gifts that come with the gift of salvation. Can you imagine that? At the moment you receive salvation all 33 things are yours!

– 24 –

Today we want to talk about only one of the extra things we receive with salvation. If you have been listening carefully to the last three lessons, you will remember that we have been learning about forgiveness. And forgiveness is one of the 33 wonderful gifts of which we have been speaking.

Show Illustration #14

If you were to receive a gift all nicely wrapped in cloth and you opened it and found a cross inside, what would you think of at once? You would remember that the Lord Jesus Christ died on a cross. Why did He die? He died as the perfect substitute for our sins. When we believe that Jesus died for us, and when we receive from God His free gift of salvation, God immediately forgives all our sins.

Forgiveness is included in the salvation gift. It is for you and me. It is for everyone who will believe that Jesus Christ is the Son of God and receive Him as Saviour. Our sinful hearts, darkened by sin, are at once made clean. That cleansing is forgiveness.

If a man robs a house, does he do it in the daytime when everyone can see him? Not usually. He chooses the nighttime darkness for his robbery. Long ago God caused it to be written in His Book that men love darkness rather than light, because their deeds are evil. "For everyone that does evil hates the light." (See John 3:19, 20.) Also in His Word we read, "God is light, and in Him is no darkness at all" (1 John 1:5).

Our hearts are full of sin. That sin is darkness. It is when we learn how perfect and holy God is, that we recognize how sinful we are. But God wants to forgive our sin. Does that mean He willingly overlooks our sin? Indeed not! God says, "The wages of sin is death" (Romans 6:23). That death is separation from God forever and forever. But God made man so that He and man could be together forever. And He wants us to be with Him in His home, Heaven. There can be no sin in Heaven. And we are all sinners. He loves us so much that, long before we were ever born, He caused His Son to take the death punishment for our sins. The Bible says it this way, "God proved His love toward us in that, while we were yet sinners, Christ died for us" (Romans 5:8). "All we like sheep have gone astray; we have turned every one to his own way; and the Lord [God] has laid on Him [the Lord Jesus] the sin of us all" (Isaiah 53:6).

So, when we receive Christ Jesus the Lord, we have His salvation gift. And that includes a forgiven heart, a heart that is new, clean, and pure. (See Ezekiel 11:19.)

2. GOD PROVIDED FORGIVENESS FOR THOSE WHO LIVED BEFORE THE LORD JESUS
Leviticus 16

What about the people who lived hundreds of years before the Lord Jesus? Could they be forgiven of their sins? Yes. But they had to offer sacrifices–many sacrifices. Those sacrifices were substitutes which died in the place of the sinner. The substitute could have been a lamb, an ox, a goat, or–if the sinner was very poor–a bird. Whatever the sacrifice was, it had to be perfect. The man took his substitute sacrifice to the tabernacle, the special place where the people of God worshiped Him. The priest killed the animal, placed it on the altar to be burned and poured its blood on the altar. As the sacrifice was offered the man asked God to forgive his sins. God heard and answered the prayer of the man, and his sins were forgiven because he had sacrificed as God had commanded. (Read the first seven chapters of Leviticus.)

Once a year (on the day of atonement) in obedience to the command of God, two goats were brought to the house of God. One was killed. Its blood was sprinkled at various places in the tabernacle, to remind the people that without shedding of blood, no sin could be forgiven. (See Leviticus 17:11; Romans 3:23-25; Hebrews 9:22.)

Show Illustration #15

The other goat brought to the house of God that day was known as the scapegoat. The priest of the house of God put his hand on the head of the live goat and confessed over it all the sins of the people. Then a man led that scapegoat out into the wilderness–a land where no one lived–and let it go. That goat was never seen again. (Read all about this in Leviticus 16.) The sins of the sinner were sent away. (See Hebrews 9:26.) The sinner was separated from his sins. He was forgiven! That was the way God commanded it should be done before His Son came to earth.

When the Lord Jesus offered Himself as the perfect sacrifice for sin, He died once–and He died for all. (See Hebrews 9:28; 10:12.) He proved He was God the Son by rising from the dead. Since the death and resurrection of our Lord Jesus Christ, animal sacrifices have no value. There is nothing man can bring to God to obtain forgiveness of sin. He cannot earn forgiveness no matter how good he is. There is only one way that man can have forgiveness of sin, and that is by accepting it as a free gift from God, through faith in the sacrifice of the Lord Jesus Christ. Everyone who truly believes Him to be the Son of God and sincerely receives Him as Saviour, is forgiven his sins and receives eternal life. (Read John 1:12; John 3:16; Ephesians 1:7.)

3. GOD PROVIDES FORGIVENESS FOR CHRISTIANS WHEN THEY CONFESS THEIR SINS TO HIM
1 John 1:9

Perhaps you are wondering what happens when a child of God sins. He has been truly born into the family of God. But he does something that is wrong. And that wrong thing is sin. A child of God should not sin, but he does. Can he be forgiven? When a Christian sins he is still a child of God–just as a boy or girl is still a child of an earthly father, even when he or she sins. But just as a sinning child and his father do not enjoy being together, so the sinning child of God does not enjoy happy fellowship with God.

Show Illustration #16a

It is as if a dark cloud comes between the believer and his Lord. Our sins separate us from God. Our sins cause His face to be hidden. (See Isaiah 59:2.) The joy of living is gone.

When Jesus died He took the punishment for *all* sins–sins we did before we were saved and sins we do after we are saved. So the child of God who has sinned should confess his sins to God. God has promised to forgive him. (See 1 John 1:9.) This forgiveness restores the child of God to fellowship with his Lord.

Show Illustration #16b

The cloud that had been between them is removed when the child of God confesses his sin to his Father God and forsakes that sin. When we walk in the light, as He is in the light, we have fellowship with God and He has fellowship with us, and the blood of Jesus Christ, His Son, keeps cleansing us from all sin. (See 1 John 1:7.)

Is everything right between you and God? Or is there some sin you should confess to Him? He is waiting and willing to forgive you if you will tell Him about it. He knows what sins you have committed. But you will never know the joy of His forgiveness until you name your sins to Him and tell Him you are truly sorry for them.

What a joy it is to have the gift of salvation–the gift that includes another gift: forgiveness!